MARGARET MEEK

HOW
Texts
Teach
What
Readers
Learn

THE THIMBLE PRESS

First published 1988
Reprinted twice 1988
Reprinted 1989; reprinted twice 1990
Reprinted 1992, 1993, 1994, 1995, 1996, 1997
1998, 1999, 2001, 2002, 2003, 2004, 2006, 2009

Printed by Lightning Source from 2011

ISBN 978 0 903355 23 0

How Texts Teach What Readers Learn

MARGARET MEEK

This booklet is a workshop rather than an essay or a lecture. To make the most of it you should refer to the texts – in most cases, books for children or young people – which I have used to illustrate the central points. You will find a list of these at the end, as well as some other interesting books to which I've referred because they have helped my thinking.

Everyone knows that the most significant things about reading are the most obvious. When Frank Smith first said that children learn to read by reading, we all agreed. We even felt that something had been revealed to us. In fact, good readers have always taken that for granted. Our commonsense notions of skill and expertise tell us that those who are good at something – making pastry or money, playing golf or bridge or the violin, or inventing computer programs – achieve mastery by practice, pleasure and persistence. Reading is no different from anything else we learn, except perhaps in that we really have to learn to do it if we are to be recognized by others as someone who can learn.

By reminding us of what we know, Frank Smith reclaimed reading for learners, freed teachers from enslavement to pedagogic methodology, and let us rediscover reading as something with language as its core. It then followed that children's aptitude for learning language, early and well, guaranteed that reading and writing are obvious, social things to do in any community where written language is part of our social function as human beings.[1]

There are many more obvious things which successful readers learn without ever being taught. So obvious are they, we seem to have missed them out of our accounts of reading and reading instruction. Most of what now follows is a list of the ordinary things that readers do without seeming to have learned them as lessons. If we look at these a little more closely than we are wont, they may turn out to be less ordinary than we first believed. If it is also true that readers learn them without reading instruction, perhaps we shall discover more about the constituent parts of the reading process.

Begin with yourself. Try to put together your autobiography in reading. (If you don't want to do it now, save it for a ruminant moment, a walk, or a way of escaping into your head in a boring meeting.) What can you remember of learning to read? Who was with you, where did it happen, what did you do? Summon up your best recollections and you will probably remember two things above all others – the difficulties and successes you had on your way, and the important turning points in your understanding of what reading was all about. Ask yourself why you are interested in reading. Scan your present reading habits. (No guilt, please, about the pile of unread books beside your bed.) Then ask yourself what you think these recollections will tell you that you think you don't know about reading. The only necessary condition for this exercise is that you should tell yourself what you already know you know, as if you were thinking of it for the first time. What comes clearly and easily to mind?

I see myself in a Scottish village primary school indus-
triously pleasing my teacher with my rendering of *Little
Red Hen, Chicken Licken* and *The Three Billy Goats Gruff.*
My grandparents, all of them, read to me and told me
stories – the endless ramifications of Scottish history and
legend which I believed had happened in their lifetime
instead of centuries before, if at all. My childhood
Sundays clanged with pulpit readings of the Authorized
Version of the Bible, *Pilgrim's Progress, Paradise Lost,*
heroic accounts of African missionaries. The weekdays,
cold and dark in the wartime winter, were a muddle of
whatever was around, Grimm, Scott, *The People's Friend.*
Reading was a form of displaced action for an asthmatic;
I could talk about things as if they had happened to me.
That I was 'good' at reading never crossed my mind, but
I liked the approval which linked pleasure and virtue. I
could not understand, when many years later I first met
someone who had never learned to read, why the process
could be so difficult. The shock of recognition which
brought all of this back was my first reading of Sartre's
autobiographical account of his early adventures in his
grandfather's library. Read it if you can; the book is
called *Words*[2].

What I next have to say will be difficult to believe. In
all of the books I have read about reading and teaching
reading there is scarcely a mention about *what* is to be
read. Books are, as the saying goes, taken as read in
discussions about reading teaching. The reading experts,
for all their understanding about 'the reading process',
treat all text as the neutral substance on which the
process works, as if the reader did the same things with
a poem, a timetable, a warning notice. They know this

isn't the case, but somehow the differentiation between reading a threatening letter, a file, or 'the mind's construction in the face' isn't regarded as part of what the reader does.

Not only that, these experts often fail to remind themselves that reading doesn't happen in a vacuum. The social conditions and surroundings are important too. For so long we have been inclined to think of reading as a silent solitary activity that we have neglected those things that are part of our reading together. People singing hymns in church are usually reading the words. Their social reading is different from that of the unemployed scanning notices in an employment centre. The reading process has always to be described in terms of texts and contexts as well as in terms of what we think readers actually do.

My disquiet about reading experts is that they decontextualize reading in order to describe it. They are casual about texts. Those whom I want to call 'expert readers' – critics, subject specialists, writers, English professors, publisher's editors and text consultants – make the same kind of mistake. They believe that there exists a group of the well-read who have a common background of texts which they all know and to which reference can be made at all times with common understanding by those 'in the know'. But they have very little curiosity about how readers in their specialism *come to know* how to read the texts of their subject. I guess that any doctor, chemist, physicist, medievalist, will tell you that they did nothing different from the reading most people do, except that their texts were special. That's obvious.

My main point is very simple. We learned to read,

competently and sensitively, because we gave ourselves what Sartre called 'private lessons', by becoming involved in what we read. We also found we could share what we read with other people, our friends, our colleagues, our opponents, even, when we argued with them. The reading lessons weren't part of a course of reading, except of the course we gave ourselves in our interactions with texts. If we can at this point acknowledge the importance of these untaught lessons, I think we should look at them more closely, beginning with the beginners.

How the book works, how the story goes

Most children come to school with a crop of reader-like behaviours and an awareness of what they expect reading to be like. They can distinguish makes of motor cars, road signs, wrappers on favourite chocolate bars. If someone has read to them, they can turn pages, tell a story from pictures, recognize advertisements on television and know that print is common in their world. If they haven't had much experience of books, there are still other 'literacy events' in their lives[3].

Many early reading skills can be missed by teachers whose training has been strictly geared to 'schooling' literacy. Teachers are naturally concerned about what pupils have to learn and their responsibility for teaching these things, so they sometimes undervalue what the children have already discovered about writing and reading. If there is no place or chance for beginners to demonstrate what they can do, what they know will never be part of their teachers' awareness.

Any significant reading research I have done rests on my having treated anecdotes as evidence. Take the case of young Ben, who had been 'offered' to one of my students as a beginner in need of extra attention because of his slow progress with the phonics check list. The student and I picked him up in the school corridor and went into a quiet corner to look at the new book for which I happened to need just such a reader – a review copy of *Rosie's Walk* by Pat Hutchins. We read it together.

First we looked at the cover and talked about the hen, the fox, the bees, and the trees with apples and pears. Ben was the leader in this discussion. He recognized the hen coop, the windmill, the farm buildings, the sun and the cloud ('There might be rain'). All of these are represented in the formal terms of the artist's design for the page; there is no attempt at realism, the fruit hangs in rows and the landscape is stylized. Yet we seemed to talk naturally about Rosie 'living' in the hen coop, despite the fact that Ben's London is far from a farm. I doubt that he had ever seen a windmill and he had never encountered a fox. Yet he picked out the elements and seemed to anticipate something of what the story might be about.

Before we opened the book there was a kind of tacit agreement by Ben that Rosie the hen might be a suitable protagonist for a tale. As her creator draws her, she is; her antecedents stretch back beyond Chaucer's Petelote, whom she resembles. Do you agree with me so far that these are reading lessons? If so, how do we come to know the character in a story whose fortunes we are to follow? Is it not in the repeated encounter on each page with the recognizable object or person? If so, then going on seems to be the best thing to do, page-turning to see 'what happens next'. Again, we've always known that, but forgotten how we learned. Where our sympathies are engaged there comes a cohesion of textual concern, even when the text is pictures. Rosie is a continuing presence; so is the fox, although his name is never once recorded in print; he is never mentioned.

When we open the page at the first two-page spread Rosie is in her coop at the left-hand side – where the reader's eyes naturally go if books aren't an entire novelty. Beyond her, on the right-hand page, is the farm, now with more buildings, and beyond it a cornfield, a distant goat, a tractor, a cart and beehives. There is no sign of the fox. The print on this page is *Pat Hutchins, ROSIE'S WALK, The Bodley Head, London, Sydney, Toronto.* Most accomplished readers turn this page, taking the conventions of publishing for granted. My clever student read the words out and we talked about where books are made. Ben said this was the third time he'd seen the title; he recognized it. Explaining Pat Hutchins took a little longer but the first-edition hardback has her picture on the back flap. That someone wrote the story and drew the pictures was a new idea for Ben; he wondered if he could see her. We said he might, for she too lived in London. As this wasn't an instructional situation in his eyes he knew he could tell us to turn the page, which we did and found the same words again, this time in tiny print with the publisher's address and the date. When did you learn that you don't read these words as part of the story?

On the facing page we next read: 'For Wendy and Stephen'. Here Ben was quickly alerted. 'I know that says Wendy,' he said. 'Her peg is next to mine. And I know Stephen, that's his name.' So we embedded this successful recognition (called 'world to text' by the experts) in the idea that authors and artists make books for children they know, but other children can read them.

If you are already bored by these details you might want to stop here, but not before I suggest that understanding authorship, audience, illustration and iconic interpretation are part of the ontogenesis of 'literary competences'[4]. To learn to read a book, as distinct from simply recognizing the words on the page, a young reader has to become both the teller (picking up the author's view and voice) and the told (the recipient of the story, the interpreter). This symbolic interaction is learned early. It is rarely, if ever, taught, except in so far as an adult stands in for the author by giving the text a 'voice' when reading to the child. Wendy and Stephen are replaced by other nameless children, in this case thousands of them, whose interpretations of the words and pictures may be as numerous, but are scarcely ever inquired into or understood for what they are. Ben knew Wendy and Stephen and he found their names in the book. That was what we knew, but we were sure there was more to know about the nature of his understanding.

The next bit is easier if you have the text in front of you. If you haven't, you can read it now: *Rosie the hen went for a walk across the yard around the pond over the haycock past the mill through the fence under the beehives and got back in time for dinner.* There are 32 words in one sentence and 27 pages of pictures. One word, 'haycock', is different in the North American text where it is 'haystack'. No one now speaks of haycocks; they have almost disappeared from our fields. But the word is familiar in a special sense to those children who recite 'Little Boy Blue'. Rosie's actual walk is described in the pictures in the terms of the size of the trees, the nearness or distancing of the goat and the windmill. A rake, a pond, a haycock, a bag of flour hanging out of the mill, beehives and a group of carts become traps for Rosie's pursuer, the fox. The words to be read reflect a quiet stroll. They are balanced by an expression of knowing insouciance on Rosie's face. Does she know he's there? That's a secret, but the reader decides. Rosie never looks behind where all the action is. The fox, with his eyes constantly trained on Rosie, falls a victim to every hazard until he is stung by the bees into retreat.

Ben enjoyed the book so much that we read it four times more. By the end of the afternoon he could tell the story and nearly match the words, so we said he could read it by himself. I don't mind if you say he had 'just memorized it'. My recollection of and conviction about this encounter is that Ben had a genuine reading experience which made up for the disappointment, the exclusion, the failure with the phonics check list. He had been in the company of readers who welcomed him as one of them; he had met an artist–author whose text had helped him to learn significant reading lessons. At the end he *possessed* the text, so that even when I took the book away with me to write about it, I took his reading with me as part of my understanding, and left him with the story to tell to someone else. He had also learned how a story goes in a book; that is, the reader tells it to himself, and every time he went back to the beginning, there it was again. Yet every reading yielded something more.

Because our concern is with the interaction of young

readers with texts, we may pass over too quickly the skill
and understanding which underlie the making of picture
books. We take the simplicity of the words for granted.
Rosie's Walk seems simple; it's a classical story
(beginning, middle, end) with clear antecedents in every
little red hen back to Aesop. But each double-page
spread with its three words of text is full of possibilities.
At 'over the haycock' there are terrified mice, a static
tethered goat, the fox leaping so near to Rosie. (The
reader has to 'read' the scratch marks that indicate
jumping.) On the next page the fox is buried in the hay;
there's a different expression on the face of the goat,
Rosie is walking on. This pattern comes four times. By
the time the reader gets to 'through the fence' he or she
knows to look ahead to spot the next obstacle. But on
this occasion the author has changed the rules. The fox
and the reader have ignored the empty cart which the
jumping fox tips so that it knocks over the beehives; not
exactly what we expected, but there as a possibility from
the very first picture.

By this time you may have had enough of Rosie, but
young readers make us patient. Let me summarize what
rereadings of this famous walk tell me about what is
there to encourage the emergence of children's 'literary
competences', and to establish, for me at least, the
necessary connections of literacy and literature. Begin
with the testimony of one of my Canadian colleagues
who had introduced Rosie and the fox to a reader of
Ben's age. Pointing to the fox he said: 'Who is that?'
'McDonald Big Ears' was the prompt reply. Thus we can
say that a page in a picture book is an icon to be
contemplated, narrated, explicated by the viewer. It
holds the story until there is a telling. So in the beginning

the words are few; the story happenings are in the pictures which form the polysemic text. The reader has to learn which of the pictorial events carries the line of the story, while each rereading shows that other things can also be taken into account. Gradually the reader learns that the narration is made up of words and pictures, together. The essential lesson of *Rosie's Walk* depends on there being no mention of the fox, but the reader knows that there would be no story without him. Nowhere but in a reader's interaction with a text can this lesson be learned. It is a lesson we take with us from wherever we first learned it to our understanding of Jane Austen.

How do children distinguish the heroine from the villain? How does an author 'recruit' their imagination and 'sustain their emotional regard', or rather how do they let her?[5]. What do they presuppose will happen, and what, exactly, is the satisfaction of the happy ending that Tolkien calls the 'eucatastrophe'? Is it an evaluation of the rightness of things that one comes to expect in a story when it is less evident in life itself? If so, where does this moral judgement come from, if not from games with rules? Is reading an elaborate game with rules? What relation has this game with rules to children's deep play and risk taking? Some of these questions can be answered by watching children's interactions with texts. My contention is that reading demands explanations beyond the information given about the surface features of language, important as that undoubtedly is.

One thing more. In all children's stories there are cultural features which locate them in a tradition. *Rosie's Walk* is a tale in the tradition of Western Europe. There is evidence that its counterparts exist in other cultures. We have passed beyond the monocultural nature of literature and literacy, so now we need to know how it is read where the text is in languages other than English.

If some of the foregoing has made sense, you should now want to read books written or made by those who take children seriously as readers. Artists and writers have a vested interest in the young because they have innocent eyes, language in the making, fewer presuppositions about the predictable and less experience of established conventions of narrative. They can be counted on as allies by virtue of their curiosity and a huge desire to learn how the world works. In addition, children's picture books are international currency; the texts are more easily translated than most. The tradition of modernism is strong. Using Bruner's metaphor again we can see that the artist or storyteller 'recruits' children's imaginations by presenting them with the familiar in a new guise, or by making a 'logical' extension of the real. When Bear in Anthony Browne's story goes for a walk he takes his pencil and draws himself out of trouble. Innovations are common in children's books because they are seen as forms of diversion. In his story about Bear, Anthony Browne's stylized jungle has flowers and plants with faces and ties (yes, *ties*), which children usually notice before adults do. Skilful makers of children's books exploit this freedom on behalf of their readers who are entering new discourses. As we have just seen they create patterns and vary them. The reader enjoys both the security of the familiar and the shock of novelty. Sometimes the critics are reproached by the artists for their failure to understand that they are dealing with the descendants of Blake, Hogarth, Caldecott and Tenniel.

Reading secrets

John Burningham's picture books are reading adventures with deep reading secrets. *Mr Gumpy's Outing* appears at first to be that most ancient of story kinds, the cumulative tale, which owes its success to the simple trick of building a story one step, and, in a book, one page-turning at a time.

> This is Mr Gumpy.
> Mr Gumpy owned a boat and his house was by a river.
> One day Mr Gumpy went out in his boat.
>   'May we come with you?' said the children.
>   'Yes,' said Mr Gumpy,
> 'if you don't squabble.'

That is how traditional storytelling dialogue works. Now it takes over the narration.

> 'Can I come along, Mr Gumpy?' said the rabbit.
> 'Yes, but don't hop about.'

The cat, the dog, the pig, the sheep, the chickens, the calf, in turn, ask Mr Gumpy's permission to board his boat. They are given leave to join the others on condition that their behaviour is decorous. Each animal makes the same request and is given the same answer; that is, the meaning stays the same but the form of the language varies.

> 'Have you a place for me?' said the sheep.
> 'Yes, but don't keep bleating.'

15

'Can you make room for me?' said the calf.
'Yes, if you don't trample about.'

'May I join you, Mr Gumpy?' said the goat.
'Very well, but don't kick.'

The reading lessons, about how dialogue appears on a page, the formal ways of making requests, the way the sentences appear on a page, go hand in hand with what children have already begun to discover about language as 'a rich and adaptable instrument for the realisation of intentions'.[6] But there is more:

'May I come, please, Mr Gumpy?' said the pig.
'Very well, but don't muck about.'

'Can we come too?' said the chickens.
'Yes, but don't flap,' said Mr Gumpy.

I'd say this is the most important lesson of all, learned early and relearned every day, as each one of us stretches our language to reconstruct, remake, extend and understand our experience of living in social contact with each other. When we want to make new meanings we need metaphor. Here the young reader discovers that the admonitions 'don't flap' and 'don't muck about' are two-sided phrases with bilateral meanings. In the context of Mr Gumpy's boat, the words *mean more than they say*.

In a later book, *Granpa*, John Burningham exploits this dialogic game even more subtly. He leaves gaps in the text to be filled with the metaphors of his paintings of the seasons which suggest the passing of time, over a year in the narrative, over the lifetime of Granpa. The text is entirely the conversation of a little girl and her grandfather. They talk about flowers in the greenhouse, the possibility of catching whales when they go fishing, what happened when Granpa was young, what they might do when he recovers from feeling unwell. The resonances of the simplest of dialogue turn-taking are about where babies come from, what is the difference between girls and boys, how memory works, how stories are to be read, what is possible, what is death and loss.

In *Come Away from the Water, Shirley* Burningham uses two modes of narration simultaneously. On the first page we see an only child and her (elderly?) parents arriving on a pebbled British beach with deckchairs and a picnic basket. Thereafter, on the left-hand page, we see the parents, seated. The text is on this side only. It consists of phrases British children have heard since sea bathing became our annual endurance test, reflecting here the unadventurousness of adults – *Of course it's far too cold for swimming, Shirley . . . Mind you don't get any of that filthy tar on your nice new shoes . . . You won't bring any of that smelly seaweed home, will you, Shirley?*

The facing pages are full of action. The reader sees Shirley and her imaginary dog rowing out to meet a boatload of pirates who make the adventurous pair walk the plank. They escape by diving into the sea, the dog with a treasure map in its mouth. They dig up the treasure and, crowned with gold, sail back just as Shirley's mother on the opposite page is saying 'Good heavens. Just look at the time. We're going to be late if we don't hurry.'

You will already have grasped that the artist uses the

17

conventions of realism to convey the life-to-text nature of the portrayal of the parents, with the thermos flasks and father sleeping under his newspaper. And we know just how the words sound if we have ever been at the beach or on a picnic during draughty, changeable August. Across the page Shirley is free to be adventurous in the ways that books and stories have taught her. The surprise for the reader, and the reading lesson, lies in the discovery of the two kinds of storytelling side by side. To be a reader you have to learn the conventions of both. Burningham is suggesting that what seems real in stories is just as conventional as what seems fantastic. What matters is to know the rules of the game the author is playing. Shirley does not bring her gold back to her mother. She knows which things are appropriate in which contexts.

Lessons in discourse

If you have read Shirley Brice Heath you will know that fantasy in texts for children is a social as well as a literary understanding[1]. My feeling is that the nature of 'made up' stories is not well enough understood by those who are confronted by the strength of imagination in childhood, when the inner and outer realities are closer together. Burningham's book shows how texts teach how they are to be read, so that there is no problem about which of the two stories is true. They both are.

Children quickly learn the rules for 'how things work around here'. Having done so, in behaviour and language, they know that the rules can be broken, by parody for example. There are alternative versions of nursery rhymes, Christmas carols, national hymns, which never find their way into books, all of which show that when they have learned the rules, children know how to subvert them. A joke is often the best reading test.

The authors who exploit their art, and the illustrators who make pictures with secrets, link what children know, partly know, and are learning about the world, to ways of presenting the world in books. These presentations are lifelike, that is, the reader senses their relation to psychological reality. But they are also scandalous, excessive, daring possibilities that the real world, the world of adults, might not endure, but which are real to children. Look for the picture books of Edward Ardizzone, John Burningham, Anthony Browne, Quentin Blake, Shirley Hughes, Janet and Allan Ahlberg, and of course, Maurice Sendak. Read them with your most adult awareness of life and literature and text, and you will see that the invitations they offer to young readers are far from infantile. Children who encounter such books learn many lessons that are hidden for ever from those who move directly from the reading scheme to the worksheet.

Compare the textual variety of children's picture books with that of reading schemes. You will see how the interactions made possible by skilled artists and writers far outweigh what can be learned from books made up by those who offer readers no excitement, no challenge, no real help. Let children talk to you about what they see in the pictures; they look more closely than their skipping and scanning elders. Don't explain everything; leave some of the artist-author's secrets for another time. What texts teach is a process of discovery for readers, not a programme of instruction for teachers.

Clubs, networks and spies

Frank Smith says readers belong to a club. I think they are members of networks, sometimes like spies. They don't all read the same books, but they know the people who like the books they like, and they also know the groups they might like to belong to. They look out for the books that other children like, and they reread old favourites. But it isn't so easy to find yourself in a familiar network as it was when there were fewer texts in school. We all read the same ones in my day. Now the number of children's books published each year would take a seven-year-old until seventy to read.

When I read with inexperienced readers I find that their difficulties lie not in the words but in understanding something that lies behind the words, embedded in the sense. It's usually an oblique reference to something the writer takes for granted that the reader will understand, so that the new text will mean more than it says. Imagine a smart detective standing over a corpse and remarking 'Curiouser and curiouser', where a phrase from *Alice in Wonderland* is set into another book as if to say 'This is a well-read detective', or in order to draw a parallel with *Alice*. It's a very ancient habit to make texts polysemic. With Chaucer and Shakespeare it wasn't plagiarism or showing off but a form of tribute or flattery. With modern novelists it might be anything from crossword puzzles to irony. Readers sometimes feel they are really rewriting the story as they read it. Barthes calls some of this 'writerly' text. To read writerly text you have to do at least half of the work.

It doesn't sound like something you expect beginning readers to be good at. Well, again they take lessons. Most people have verses from childhood, groups of words, sayings, rhymes, in their heads that are part of the texture of the language, spoken or written. As a writer you could count on children knowing, say, Humpty Dumpty, or Old Mother Hubbard, Jack and Jill, Cinderella perhaps. That's what Janet and Allan Ahlberg do in *Each Peach Pear Plum*. The young reader doesn't have to know about Tom Thumb to be able to read the words 'I spy Tom Thumb'; the invitation from the artist is to find him in the picture. But if the beginner has heard of him before, in a rhyme or in another book, there are two kinds of finding: one of the boy hiding in the picture, the other of the fact that Tom Thumb is also known to the Ahlbergs in the way that we all say we know Jane Eyre or Billy Bunter.

Experts tell us that the lucky children are those who are read to. If they know stories or rhymes by heart, they bring the words *to* the page when they read for themselves. They discover that you can play with language in both speech and writing, and they also learn not to expect the same sense from 'Diddle diddle dumpling, my son John' as from stories about a first day in school.

The most important single lesson that children learn from texts is *the nature and variety of written discourse*, the different ways that language lets a writer tell, and the many and different ways a reader reads. Go back again to your own learning. How did you know when you were reading a joke? Didn't you practise asking them before you fully understood the puns of the 'Knock, knock' game? Wasn't it the conspiratorial feeling of the exchanges that pleased you? Irony – not saying quite what you mean – is likewise socially learned. We saw the beginning of it in *Rosie's Walk*.

As the learning goes on: the transition stage

Experienced literary critics, those who never read children's books now but whose memories are laden with the rhymes of childhood, tell us that there is enough childhood lore in all literature to be fed into stories at all stages of learning to read, right up to Joyce's *Ulysses*. Those who know how to recognize bits and pieces of other texts in what they read find it is like the discovery of old friends in new places. They feel they are sharing a secret with the writer (that conspiratorial feeling again). They become 'insiders' in the network.

Children enter the intertext of literature, oral and written, very early; as soon as they know some nursery rhymes, in fact, and later, when they have amassed the lore of the school playground, they are able to recognize in their reading what has been in their memories for some time.

The best example of what I am trying to explain is another book by the Ahlbergs. (They have a special kind of insight into the part the oral tradition plays in the lives of children.) It's called *The Jolly Postman, or Other People's Letters*. Readers of about seven or eight enjoy it because they know that letters are good things to get, and other people's letters have secrets you're not supposed to read. In the book the Jolly Postman, who rides a bicycle, takes letters to the homes of some characters from nursery

22

rhymes. The connecting story is told in rhyme. But the intrigue lies in the fact that some pages of the book are envelopes containing the actual letters which the reader takes out and reads. So here is Goldilocks, writing to apologize to the Three Bears for breaking and entering. The Wicked Witch gets a flyer from Hobgoblin Supplies Ltd, who make special offers for Hallowe'en boots, deadly lampshades, newts, boy powder, and books of foul spells. A publisher sends to H.R.H. Cinderella a little book of her recent adventures specially prepared on the occasion of her wedding. Here is my favourite, from solicitors Meeny, Miny, Mo & Co. to B.B. Wolf, Esq., c/o Grandma's Cottage, Horner's Corner:

```
Dear Mr Wolf,

We are writing to you on behalf of our
client, Miss Riding-Hood, concerning her
grandma.  Miss Hood tells us that you
are presently occupying her grandma's
cottage and wearing her grandma's clothes
without this lady's permission.

Please understand that if this harassment
does not cease, we will call in the Official
Woodcutter, and - if necessary - all the
King's horses and all the King's men.

On a separate matter, we must inform you
that Messrs. Three Little Pigs Ltd. are
now firmly resolved to sue for damages.
Your offer of shares in a turnip or
apple-picking business is declined, and
all this huffing and puffing will get
you nowhere.

Yours sincerely,

Harold Meeny

H Meeny
```

Inside the verse text of *The Jolly Postman*, quite literally *inside*, in the envelopes, are texts whose conventions are drawn from the world of actual literacy events: personal letters, publishing, the law, travel brochures and advertising. The contents refer to the world of the fairy story. The Ahlbergs never make mistakes in reaching their readers, so they know that this intricate intertext will be read by those who are ready to read it.

On the surface, intertext can seem to be a kind of literary joke; underneath, it is a very serious business, part of the whole intricate network of words which mean more than they say. Readers of *The Jolly Postman* enter the world of *If on a Winter's Night a Traveller*. They also find themselves in the network of political propaganda and other less honourably subversive texts.

This intertextuality cannot be a feature of the reading scheme, which offers words to be read only in order to reinforce lessons that are taught *about* reading rather than learned *by* reading. The result is a divergence in competence and understanding between young readers who have entered the reading network through the multiple meanings of polysemic texts and those who may have practised only on the reductive features of words written to be 'sounded out' or 'recognized'. Those who have had only the latter experience often feel that they are missing something when they read a text which they know means more than it says.

Examples from middle childhood and longer texts

We are talking about *narrations*, ways that the tellers of stories in books teach children how to read them. We have looked at some of the ways in which modern artists make storytelling in picture books as intriguing as the seductive narratives of television. We are bound, as a result, to acknowledge the power of images – that is, non-verbal representations of ideas (connected, of course, with imagination) – to be, in the early stages of reading, as important as words. Think of the appeal of Raymond Briggs's *The Snowman*. Evidence from research emphasizes the importance of images. It's schooling, and the teaching of reading as a concern with words alone, that puts into our heads the notion that books with pictures are a preliterate form of storytelling, while all the time the very force of television shows us this is not the case.

What counts in children's climbing up through their school years is the ability confidently to tackle longer and longer stretches of continuous prose, in both reading and writing. But, like adults, children take time out. Outside the classroom, the library, the bookish they find the popular culture of childhood in comics. Looking back at the debates which have arranged around these productions I'm surprised that we have ignored for so long the reading skills they taught our readers. The classic comic demands that two interpretations be made together, of pictures and text. Balloon dialogue (and the one with the wavy line for 'thinks'), inset sketches, drawing 'asides', together with the reader's impulse to keep the story going while taking all this in, should have alerted us sooner to the ways by which the young reader becomes both the teller and the told, what Bakhtin calls 'the dialogic imagination'.[7]

And this is reading in its social context; readers of comics swop them, act out the farces which they enjoy, and know that the adults are in two minds about their worth. It is well nigh impossible to read a comic *to* a child. To read one *with* a child an adult has to be accepted as a peer, and even this is thought of as a kind of intrusion.

In *Chips and Jessie* Shirley Hughes combines as many of the discourse forms as any nine-year-old will have encountered. In devising an intriguing form of storytelling she mixes the conventions of the comic with 'straight' bookish text, and thereby shows what pictures can do that text cannot. For example, overlapping events that occur at the same time can be depicted simultaneously but have to be related sequentially. Her skill in exploiting this mixed form can be seen in the episode of Chico, the hamster brought home from school who escapes and is lost. There is a lull in the rush of events at the point where Chico has been replaced by another hamster and all seems well. The formal story text says:

> That evening Chips and Jessie were sitting on the kitchen table at Chips' house. Mum had taken Gloria to visit a friend and Grandpa was working in his garden shed. It was getting dark. Jessie was keeping Chips company by telling him all about a very spooky film she had seen on TV. It was about a man who had been locked up in a terrible prison on an island from which no one could escape, even though he had done nothing wrong.

Above the heads of Chips and Jessie are the words of their dialogue, and above that is a picture of their mental image of the prisoner and another of the island. Then,

From *Chips and Jessie* by Shirley Hughes (Bodley Head)

on the next page, as Jessie describes the prisoner scratching on the wall, the reader *sees* the missing Chico in the rim of the picture as he makes his way down behind the kitchen wall towards the taps and the sink.

This particular kind of multiconsciousness, apparently so natural in childhood yet culturally, and specifically, learned, is passed over as children are taught to pay attention only to words in books. The ousting of images by text has not been an unmitigated gain in the teaching of literacy, as we are only now beginning to realize.

More learning

Perhaps at this point we should remind ourselves that these are not the only lessons children learn; the stories themselves, what they are about, are also lessons of a kind, the kind that most adults are more concerned with when they talk about a book being 'suitable'.

When children read comfortably, when the rules of 'how the story goes' are quickly and familiarly settled between author and reader, reading feels easy. Readers know they can read, and authors can take their skill for granted. Teachers are so relieved that they encourage the young to go ahead as fast as they can. It's usually a good time for new readers to learn other lessons, but if they don't get the stories that help them, they are running on the spot instead of striding out.

Let's stay with the familiar kind of story for a little, the one where the hero or heroine is involved in unexpected events or suffers a temporary desolation but, in both cases, all comes right in the end. In books written in the last thirty years these tales of childhood have presented to young readers a version of being young which is optimistic and, on the whole, comfortable. There are certain tacit assumptions within them that this is what childhood is, or should be, like.

When the structure of the story is familiar, readers are free to look at other possible lessons to be learned from events they may never encounter and kinds of people who may never cross their path. Now the reader is to ask: What would I do if I found myself in that situation? Do I or do I not care for people like that? Is there a part of me that understands them?

Here begin two kinds of explorations, of the value system that prevails in the world and the one revealed in the text, and also of the way narratives handle these things, not only in the conventions of the realistic tale but also in the more metaphorical instances in folktales and legends. Readers have to confront truth/falsehood, trust/betrayal, heroism/cowardice, unselfishness/self-concern and all the other ways in which our interactions with each other are construed and presented in life and in stories. Both life and text have to be interrogated about 'the way things might be'. *Sir Gawain and the Green Knight* brings up all of these puzzles at once, but they are also present in the work of Enid Blyton and Roald Dahl, which children read with great pleasure.

'Who is the reader to become, during the time of reading?' is a powerful question from Wayne Booth.[8] We know from children's addiction to the Famous Five and their fondness for *Danny* and *Boy* that they are trying out different kinds of companionship, perhaps of those whose lives seem to involve them in more risk-taking than their own. If they read all the works of these authors, and many children do, they come to the question: 'Do I want to read about these people any more?' when someone asks them what they like or puts in their way something different. It's at this moment that the kind of telling comes into focus, a chance to read not so much about different people but to read about people differently.

Readers who read a lot soon discover what is suitable

29

or unsuitable in a story. In fiction, as in life, it is a judgement they learn to make from evidence they understand. Instead of condemning some children's stories as 'unsuitable', adults need to take time to help children talk about what they read so that they learn to express their judgements, however tentatively at first. Many a good reading lesson from an undistinguished book has been smothered by too emphatic classroom demands for the reader to pronounce immediately on characters or actions, when a time for thought might have been more helpful.

The signs of genuine reading development are hard to detect as they appear, and bear little relation to what is measured by reading tests. For me, the move from 'more of the same' to 'I might try something different' is a clear step. So is a growing tolerance of ambiguity, the notion that things are not quite what they seem, even in a fairly straightforward tale about, say, a family seaside holiday or the unexpected behaviour on the part of parents.

Two texts help me to distinguish moves in children's reading. The first is *The Iron Man* by Ted Hughes. It can be read with pleasure and understanding by children at all stages in school, from the reception class to the sixth form. This is not exaggerated praise but a serious claim, and what happens is not a smooth progression but a series of loopings back to find new awarenesses in oneself as a reader. Some of the youngest readers see as deeply into Hughes's stated intentions for the story[9] as do the oldest. The crossing point from reading and understanding 'what happens' to the Iron Man to interpreting the mythic implications comes for most children when, in answer to the question 'If we had Mr Hughes here, what would you like to ask him about his book?' the child says, 'Where did he get the idea from?' The idea is the meeting place of reader and writer, the intersection of culture and cognition; the readers are now writing as they read.

By the time they are eight, or a little later, children are generally expected to choose books for themselves. Those who know that authors help them to make sense of the story are more patient with the beginnings of books than those who expect to recognize straightaway what they have to understand. The common phrase for this process is 'getting into the story'. Practised readers tolerate uncertainty; they know that sometimes the author is building up suspense and that the puzzle will be resolved if they just keep reading. I wish I knew more about how we learn to tolerate uncertainty in our reading and what we are really doing. The poet W.H. Auden says that we go on reading books we only partly understand if they have been given to us by someone we like and we want to be thought well of by him or her.[10] Many a good tutor has let fall the title of a book, implying that of course the student will want to read it. Remember the early untaught lessons of approval and virtue? I doubt if this kind of suasion is very prevalent nowadays but surely, surely we should continue to help young readers to 'get into' books until they are confident that they need not be daunted. We needn't do more than reduce some of the uncertainty; the author will take over where we leave off.

My second special text – the best example I know of a story for readers near the end of their primary school – is one which does everything I've already mentioned. It is based on a subtle play of intertexts which a young reader will certainly 'get' and understand and thereby

31

feel confident, perhaps even superior, in the 'knowing-ness' that it produces about reading itself. It's 'William's Version' by Jan Mark. See if you have to tolerate the uncertainty of the beginning.

William and Granny were left to entertain each other for an hour while William's mother went to the clinic.

'Sing to me,' said William.

'Granny's too old to sing,' said Granny.

'I'll sing to you, then,' said William. William only knew one song. He had forgotten the words and the tune, but he sang it several times, anyway.

'Shall we do something else now?' said Granny.

'Tell me a story,' said William. 'Tell me about the wolf.'

'Red Riding Hood?'

'No, not *that* wolf, the other wolf.'

'Peter and the wolf?' said Granny.

'Mummy's going to have a baby,' said William.

'I know,' said Granny.

William looked suspicious.

'How do you know?'

'Well . . . she told me. And it shows, doesn't it?'

Publisher's note. In 'Symbolic Outlining: The Academic Study of Children's Literature' (*Signal* 53, May 1987) Margaret Meek said: 'The nature of the possible is what children learn when they discover how to use language for subversion, for re-ordering things in their heads if not in fact. The best story I know for making this clear to students of children's books is Jan Mark's "William's Version".' For readers' convenience, the full text of this story is reprinted on pages 43 to 48.

'The lady down the road had a baby. It looks like a pig,' said William. He counted on his fingers. 'Three babies looks like three pigs.'

'Ah,' said Granny. 'Once upon a time there were three little pigs. Their names were –'

'They didn't have names,' said William.

'Yes they did. The first pig was called –'

'Pigs don't have names.'

'Some do. These pigs had names.'

'No they didn't.' William slid off Granny's lap and went to open the corner cupboard by the fireplace. Old magazines cascaded out as old magazines do when they have been flung into a cupboard and the door slammed shut. He rooted among them until he found a little book covered with brown paper, climbed into the cupboard, opened the book, closed it and climbed out again. 'They didn't have names,' he said.

'I didn't know you could read,' said Granny, properly impressed.

'C–A–T, wheelbarrow,' said William.

'Is that the book Mummy reads to you out of?'

'It's my book,' said William.

'But it's the one Mummy reads?'

'If she says please,' said William.

'Well, that's Mummy's story then. My pigs have names.'

'They're the wrong pigs.' William was not open to negotiation. 'I don't want them in this story.'

'Can't we have different pigs this time?'

'No. They won't know what to do.'

'Once upon a time,' said Granny, 'there were three little pigs who lived with their mother.'

'Their mother was dead,' said William.

'Oh, I'm sure she wasn't,' said Granny.

'She was dead. You make bacon out of dead pigs. She got eaten for breakfast and they threw the rind out for the birds.'

'So the three little pigs had to find homes for themselves.'

'No.' William consulted his book. 'They had to build little houses.'

'I'm just coming to that.'

'You said they had to *find* homes. They didn't *find* them.'

'The first little pig walked along for a bit until he met a man with a load of hay.'

The story proceeds in this dialogic format, with William countering his Granny's telling of every event in the old tale with a version of his own. Granny struggles to continue the narrative. When William has diverted her at a crucial point, she says, 'Why don't you tell the story?' William then produces a green scarf called Doctor Snake. Granny tries again. William adds aleatoric interventions which he seems to find in the book he has taken from the cupboard. The final argument is about the fate of the wolf. Granny tells the traditional ending: 'and the wolf fell down the chimney and into the pan of water and was boiled and the little pig ate him for supper.' The result of this is a wild tantrum from William, who then offers his version, which you can read on page 48, beginning 'The little pig put the saucepan . . .'.

I have read this story many times in class and elsewhere. The effect is always one of great delight, but you and I know that there is deep play in this text.

William's version is older than even the tale of the three little pigs. He is 'positioned within' the story his grandmother tells; that new baby is a great threat to his identity, to his self-love. Like the story, he suffers displacement. Young readers recognize this effect even before they have the means or the understanding to explain it. In its turn the text gives them a site, a location for the pursuit of their understanding. I don't want to press too hard the notion of the 'ego as a critical construction' but Lacan's ideas[11] are germane to our coming to know how children are subjectively located in language and culture. Any consideration of texts for children has to encounter the intertext of the reader's unconscious at some stage. The reading lesson here is that texts reveal what we think we have successfully concealed even from ourselves.

Adult lessons

As we become more experienced in reading so we can become less and not more skilled. In some ways we even make one kind of reading do for all. I mean this in two ways: first, about the way we read only what we find comfortable, rushing through novels to finish the story and then going on to another one. Then, if we are reading teachers or teachers of literature, we may adopt too easily patterns of work which don't encourage us to inspect what we do. Habitual readers can become less adventurous than their skills allow. It's like driving in second gear in a high-powered car.

We can understand this if we go back again to our own reading, the kind we do with ease and pleasure. We can

35

manage most texts, the written papers which impinge on the run of our ordinary lives, because we know what they refer to and the kinds of responses that are expected from us when we fill in tax forms, write reports or take time with boring but important matters from the bank. But how often do we who teach children to read, or who read on their behalf, give ourselves reading lessons? When do we read a new novel twice, that is, if we're not going to teach it for an examination? Do we even do that when we're going to read it to a class, once to see 'what happens' and again to see if we can penetrate the secrets of 'how it's done' or 'what more is there here?'?

Children read stories they like over and over again; that's when they pay attention to the words – after they've discovered what happens. Adults, generally, go on to the next book, so that *how* we read isn't part of the consciousness we bring to texts. We usually don't need to ask because, for our comfort, it's often 'another of the same'. I find that I give myself reading lessons when I write reviews – a stringent discipline if it's done well. I admire good reviewers very much, so I don't let myself read anyone else's piece until mine is safely beyond my reach for revision. It's the writing that makes me aware of what I'm doing when I read.

I'm also very, very curious about how other people read, not least because there seems to be no end to the interpretive possibilities of some texts. Certainly, all readers bring different things *to* the text, but this makes me keener than ever to know: what makes the difference. How did we discover that certain ways of saying things are meaningful in the first place? What does the order of words on the page do to the way I look at things? Jerome Bruner says that if we ask a reader what kind of story he or she is reading we are not expecting a reply to tell us about the nature of the text but about what's happening to the reader.[5] When I asked a six-year-old which part of *The Iron Man* she liked best, she said: 'My favourite is *delicacies*.' Here's what she was remembering:

> The Iron Man gazed, and his eyes turned red. He kneeled down in the yard, he stretched out on one elbow. He picked up a greasy black stove and chewed it like a toffee. There were delicious crumbs of chrome on it. He followed that with a double-decker bedstead and the brass knobs made his eyes crackle with joy. Never before had the Iron Man eaten such delicacies.

The word summed up that whole section of visual concreteness; she brought back the picture with a word. The others in the group taking part in the discussion nodded. They knew exactly what she meant, although the chances are that their images were quite different.

Teaching lessons

Young people nowadays practise their interpretive processes mostly by watching television. They find difficulty in tolerating the slow speed of classical texts where the scene has to be set in passages of description before the action can get going. They are also less tolerant of passages of text recall, especially if there are other stories embedded in these. A visual flashback goes over the same kind of ground, literally in a flash. 'Getting into' a novel like *Huckleberry Finn* needs a fair amount of tolerance of uncertainty. How would you deal with the part where Huck is complaining that Tom Sawyer is always making up adventure games from stories he has read in books?

'I didn't see no di'monds and I told Tom Sawyer so. He said there was A-rabs there too, and elephants and things. I said why couldn't we see them, then? He said if I warn't so ignorant, but had read a book called *Don Quixote*, I would know without asking.' Huck wants real adventure while Tom re-creates book adventures for real. Later Huck and Tom have 'real' adventures which become part of the virtual experience of every reader of the book. When a novel as 'layered' as this is turned into a film the 'meanings' have to be translated into the semiotics of the visual. What disappears is not the plot, the characters or the recollection of 'what happens' but the experience of reading. Television and books are allies. I don't believe that the one drives out the other. But we need to be clearer about the kinds of 'reading' offered by both. I find I need the young to teach me as much as I think I can teach them. One of the sharpest late reading lessons I have learned is to *let* the texts teach the reader, as I would do in the case of *Huckleberry Finn*. The problem for teachers in secondary schools is to give students enough experience of different kinds of text while exploring the secrets and lessons of only some of them.

If we want to see what lessons have been learned from the texts children read, we have to look for them in what they write. Of course, they draw on the whole of their culture if we let them. We have to be alert to what comes from books as well as from life. This topic must wait for another occasion.

By this time you will have reduced my repetitive

argument to the idea that 'real' books are good reading texts for learners because they introduce children to the discourse styles of various genres. That's true, but it's not the whole story. Experimental authors are constantly changing the genres. All over the world new writers appear, writing in their English, a different cultural stream from the deep old channel of the Thames. Their narrative styles are different; they draw on different intertexts. They have their way to make. Children too have different demands. I have rested my case on narrative fiction, but every area of knowledge teaches the apprentices how people write in that domain. That's the lesson of the history book, the geography folder, the science manual, the engineering drawing. These teach their own lessons, yet we know very little about how these lessons are learned. All scientific discovery is as dramatic as the events in a novel or a film, but in the written report to the learned society the excitement must be edited out. Topic discourse, says Harold Rosen, 'covers its narrative tracks'.[12] This is another text-taught lesson.

The case for narrative fiction is best made in a short statement by Jonathan Culler, from whom I borrowed the idea of 'literary competences'. He is discussing ways of reading 'the text as an exploration of writing, of the problems of articulating a world'. He says that the job of the critic and that of every reader is 'an attempt to capture its force. The force, the power of any text, even the most unabashedly mimetic, lies in those moments which exceed our ability to categorize, which collide with our interpretive codes but nevertheless seem right'. He goes on: 'Fiction can hold together within a single space a variety of languages, levels of focus, points of view, which would be contradictory in other kinds of discourse organized towards a particular empirical end'[4].

Strange as it may seem, the reading of stories makes skilful, powerful readers who come to understand not only the meaning but also the force of texts. It is a strong defence against being victimized by the reductive power of so-called 'functional literacy'. It also makes writers.

Tailpiece

If you think that the arguments of this booklet are too impressionistic, too shallowly rooted in empirical evidence, may I direct you to the main source of my conviction. For more than five years my colleagues and I examined the reading of a group of adolescents who had been deemed to be unteachable. In fact they had learned too well too many unhelpful lessons. They had never been trusted with real texts. Their early encounters with reading had not included books as a source of pleasure, play, desire. At best they could say a few words after prompting. They had been given only conditional entry into their culture and they wanted nothing of the tyranny of literacy. We gave them real books and showed them how texts teach[13].

It is hard for anyone whose life has been enriched by books to exclude the young from this source of pleasure and serious reflection. What we have to realize is that the young have powerful allies in a host of gifted artists and writers to help them to subvert the world of their elders.

How Texts Teach . . .

Children's Books Cited in the Text

Janet and Allan Ahlberg, *Each Peach Pear Plum*, Kestrel, 1976
Janet and Allan Ahlberg, *The Jolly Postman or Other People's Letters*, Heinemann, 1986
Anthony Browne, *Bear Hunt*, Hamish Hamilton, 1978
John Burningham, *Come Away from the Water, Shirley*, Cape, 1977
John Burningham, *Granpa*, Cape, 1984
John Burningham, *Mr Gumpy's Outing*, Cape, 1970
Shirley Hughes, *Chips and Jessie*, Bodley Head, 1985
Ted Hughes, *The Iron Man*, Faber & Faber, 1968
Pat Hutchins, *Rosie's Walk*, Bodley Head, 1969
Jan Mark, 'William's Version' in *Nothing to be Afraid Of*, Viking Kestrel, 1980

References

1. Shirley Brice Heath, *Ways with Words*, Cambridge University Press, 1983.
2. Jean-Paul Sartre, *Words*, Penguin, 1969.
3. See for example Hillel Goelman, Antoinette A. Oberg and Frank Smith (editors), *Awakening to Literacy*, Exeter, N.H.: Heinemann, 1984. See also the chapters by Carol Fox and Henrietta Dombey in Margaret Meek (editor), *Opening Moves*, Bedford Way Papers No. 17, University of London Institute of Education, 1983.
4. Jonathan Culler, *Structuralist Poetics*, Routledge and Kegan Paul, 1977.
5. Jerome S. Bruner, *Actual Minds, Possible Worlds*, Harvard University Press, 1986.
6. M.A.K. Halliday, 'Relevant Models of Language' in *Educational Review*, volume 22, number 7, pages 26-34.
7. M.M. Bakhtin, *The Dialogic Imagination: Four Essays*, University of Texas Press, 1981.
8. Wayne Booth, 'Narrative as the Mold of Character' in *A Telling Exchange*, Report of the conference on Narrative held to mark the retirement of Harold Rosen, University of London Institute of Education, 1984.

9. Ted Hughes, 'Myth and Education' in *Writers, Critics and Children*, edited by Geoff Fox et al, Heinemann Educational, 1976.
10. W.H. Auden, 'Making, Knowing, Judging' in *The Dyer's Hand and Other Essays*, Faber & Faber, 1963.
11. Jacques Lacan, *Écrits: A Selection*, translated by Alan Sheridan, Tavistock Publications, 1977.
12. Harold Rosen, *Stories and Meanings*, NATE Publications, 1984.
13. Margaret Meek et al, *Achieving Literacy*, Routledge and Kegan Paul, 1983.

Acknowledgements

The facsimile letter on page 23 is reproduced from *The Jolly Postman, or Other People's Letters* by Janet & Allan Ahlberg (Heinemann).

'William's Version' is one of ten short stories in *Nothing to Be Afraid Of* by Jan Mark, illustrated by David Parkin (Viking Kestrel). One of Mr Parkin's line drawings for the story appears on page 47.

William's Version

JAN MARK

William and Granny were left to entertain each other for an hour while William's mother went to the clinic.

'Sing to me,' said William.

'Granny's too old to sing,' said Granny.

'I'll sing to you, then,' said William. William only knew one song. He had forgotten the words and the tune, but he sang it several times, anyway.

'Shall we do something else now?' said Granny.

'Tell me a story,' said William. 'Tell me about the wolf.'

'Red Riding Hood?'

'No, not *that* wolf, the other wolf.'

'Peter and the wolf?' said Granny.

'Mummy's going to have a baby,' said William.

'I know,' said Granny.

William looked suspicious.

'How do you know?'

'Well . . . she told me. And it shows, doesn't it?'

'The lady down the road had a baby. It looks like a pig,' said William. He counted on his fingers. 'Three babies looks like three pigs.'

'Ah,' said Granny. 'Once upon a time there were three little pigs. Their names were –'

'They didn't have names,' said William.

'Yes they did. The first pig was called –'

'Pigs don't have names.'

'Some do. These pigs had names.'

'No they didn't.' William slid off Granny's lap and went to open the corner cupboard by the fireplace. Old magazines cascaded out as old magazines do when they have been flung into a cupboard and the door slammed shut. He rooted among them until he found a little book covered with brown paper, climbed into the cupboard, opened the book, closed it and climbed out again. 'They didn't have names,' he said.

'I didn't know you could read,' said Granny, properly impressed.

Jan Mark

'C – A – T, wheelbarrow,' said William.

'Is that the book Mummy reads to you out of?'

'It's my book,' said William.

'But it's the one Mummy reads?'

'If she says please,' said William.

'Well, that's Mummy's story, then. My pigs have names.'

'They're the wrong pigs.' William was not open to negotiation. 'I don't want them in this story.'

'Can't we have different pigs this time?'

'No. They won't know what to do.'

'Once upon a time,' said Granny, 'there were three little pigs who lived with their mother.'

'Their mother was dead,' said William.

'Oh, I'm sure she wasn't,' said Granny.

'She was dead. You make bacon out of dead pigs. She got eaten for breakfast and they threw the rind out for the birds.'

'So the three little pigs had to find homes for themselves.'

'No.' William consulted his book. 'They had to build little houses.'

'I'm just coming to that.'

'You said they had to *find* homes. They didn't *find* them.'

'The first little pig walked along for a bit until he met a man with a load of hay.'

'It was a lady.'

'A lady with a load of hay?'

'NO! It was a lady-pig. You said *he*.'

'I thought all the pigs were little boy-pigs,' said Granny.

'It says lady-pig here,' said William. 'It says the lady-pig went for a walk and met a man with a load of hay.'

'So the lady-pig,' said Granny, 'said to the man, "May I have some of that hay to build a house?" and the man said, "Yes." Is that right?'

'Yes,' said William. 'You know that baby?'

'What baby?'

'The one Mummy's going to have. Will that baby have shoes on when it comes out?'

'I don't think so,' said Granny.

'It will have cold feet,' said William.

'Oh no,' said Granny. 'Mummy will wrap it up in a soft shawl, all snug.'

'I don't *mind* if it has cold feet,' William explained. 'Go on about the

44

lady-pig.'

'So the little lady-pig took the hay and built a little house. Soon the wolf came along and the wolf said –'

'You didn't tell where the wolf lived.'

'I don't know where the wolf lived.'

'15 Tennyson Avenue, next to the bomb-site,' said William.

'I bet it doesn't say that in the book,' said Granny, with spirit.

'Yes it does.'

'Let me see, then.'

William folded himself up with his back to Granny, and pushed the book up under his pullover.

'*I* don't think it says that in the book,' said Granny.

'It's in ever so small words,' said William.

'So the wolf said, "Little pig, little pig, let me come in," and the little pig answered, "No". So the wolf said, "Then I'll huff and I'll puff and I'll blow your house down," and he huffed and he puffed and he blew the house down, and the little pig ran away.'

'He ate the little pig,' said William.

'No, no,' said Granny. 'The little pig ran away.'

'He ate the little pig. He ate her in a sandwich.'

'All right, he ate the little pig in a sandwich. So the second little pig –'

'You didn't tell about the tricycle.'

'What about the tricycle?'

'The wolf got on his tricycle and went to the bread shop to buy some bread. To make the sandwich,' William explained, patiently.

'Oh well, the wolf got on his tricycle and went to the bread shop to buy some bread. And he went to the grocer's to buy some butter.' This innovation did not go down well.

'He already had some butter in the cupboard,' said William.

'So then the second little pig went for a walk and met a man with a load of wood, and the little pig said to the man, "May I have some of that wood to build a house?" and the man said, "Yes." '

'He didn't say please.'

' "Please may I have some of that wood to build a house?" '

'It was sticks.'

'Sticks *are* wood.'

William took out his book and turned the pages. 'That's right,' he said.

Jan Mark

'Why don't you tell the story?' said Granny.

'I can't remember it,' said William.

'You could read it out of your book.'

'I've lost it,' said William, clutching his pullover. 'Look, do you know who this is?' He pulled a green angora scarf from under the sofa.

'No, who is it?' said Granny, glad of the diversion.

'This is Doctor Snake.' He made the scarf wriggle across the carpet.

'Why is he a doctor?'

'Because he is all furry,' said William. He wrapped the doctor round his neck and sat sucking the loose end. 'Go on about the wolf.'

'So the little pig built a house of sticks and along came the wolf – on his tricycle?'

'He came by bus. He didn't have any money for a ticket so he ate up the conductor.'

'That wasn't very nice of him,' said Granny.

'No,' said William. 'It wasn't *very* nice.'

'And the wolf said, "Little pig, little pig, let me come in," and the little pig said, "No," and the wolf said, "Then I'll huff and I'll puff and I'll blow your house down," so he huffed and he puffed and he blew the house down. And then what did he do?' Granny asked, cautiously.

William was silent.

'Did he eat the second little pig?'

'Yes.'

'How did he eat this little pig?' said Granny, prepared for more pig sandwiches or possibly pig on toast.

'With his mouth,' said William.

'Now the third little pig went for a walk and met a man with a load of bricks. And the little pig said, "*Please* may I have some of those bricks to build a house?" and the man said, "Yes." So the little pig took the bricks and built a house.'

'He built it on the bomb-site.'

'Next door to the wolf?' said Granny. 'That was very silly of him.'

'There wasn't anywhere else,' said William. 'All the roads were full up.'

'The wolf didn't have to come by bus or tricycle this time, then, did he?' said Granny, grown cunning.

'Yes.' William took out the book and peered in, secretively. 'He

46

was playing in the cemetery. He had to get another bus.'

'And did he eat the conductor this time?'

'No. A nice man gave him some money, so he bought a ticket.'

'I'm glad to hear it,' said Granny.

'He ate the nice man,' said William.

'So the wolf got off the bus and went up to the little pig's house, and he said, "Little pig, little pig, let me come in," and the little pig said, "No," and then the wolf said, "I'll huff and I'll puff and I'll blow your house down," and he huffed and he puffed and he huffed and he puffed but he couldn't blow the house down because it was made of bricks.'

'He couldn't blow it down,' said William, 'because it was stuck to the ground.'

'Well, anyway, the wolf got very cross then, and he climbed on the roof and shouted down the chimney, "I'm coming to get you!" but

47

the little pig just laughed and put a big saucepan of water on the fire.'

'He put it on the gas stove.'

'He put it on the *fire*,' said Granny, speaking very rapidly, 'and the wolf fell down the chimney and into the pan of water and was boiled and the little pig ate him for supper.'

William threw himself full length on the carpet and screamed.

'He didn't! He didn't! *He didn't!* He didn't eat the wolf.'

Granny picked him up, all stiff and kicking, and sat him on her lap.

'Did I get it wrong again, love? Don't cry. Tell me what really happened.'

William wept, and wiped his nose on Doctor Snake.

'The little pig put the saucepan on the gas stove and the wolf got down the chimney and put the little pig in the saucepan and boiled him. He had him for tea, with chips,' said William.

'Oh,' said Granny. 'I've got it all wrong, haven't I? Can I see the book, then I shall know, next time.'

William took the book from under his pullover. Granny opened it and read, *First Aid for Beginners: a Practical Handbook*.

'I see,' said Granny. 'I don't think I can read this. I left my glasses at home. You tell Gran how it ends.'

William turned to the last page which showed a prostrate man with his leg in a splint; *compound fracture of the femur*.

'Then the wolf washed up and got on his tricycle and went to see his Granny, and his Granny opened the door and said, "Hello, William." '

'I thought it was the wolf.'

'It was. It was the wolf. His name was William Wolf,' said William.

'What a nice story,' said Granny. 'You tell it much better than I do.'

'I can see up your nose,' said William. 'It's all whiskery.'